THE LITTLE BLUE BOOK

KERI COOK

THE LITTLE
BLUE BOOK

A Young Woman's Guide to
Loving Who You Are

Keri Cook

To my dearest sister, Hallie. Spend your years knowing you are loved, valued, and adored. Know your worth, know there are no limits to what you can accomplish, and know that I will always be here for you.

Love, Keri

CONTENTS

CONTENTS

PREFACE

In the spirit of total transparency I feel that it is important that I explain my reasoning for the creation of this book you have resting here in your hands. I did not create this book to change the world - I did, however, write this book with the hopes that I can play a small, positive role in the lives of young women from across the world.

My desire to empower young women began while working with the Circle for Girls Foundation - an organization that mentors young women while walking them through the importance of loving themselves, establishing healthy relationships, setting safe boundaries, creating confidence, and many other important lessons. During my time with the Foundation, I discovered that there was a significant amount of young women who were not given this same opportunity. With this insight, I wanted to do what I could to try to ensure that these lessons and conversations were accessible to all young women - not just those who were able to attend our weekly gatherings.

It was through my work, where I learned that young women would come into the program having hundreds of questions that had been left unanswered. Through our discussions, I discovered that these questions were going unanswered because they aren't conventional questions. Taking it one step further - these questions are rarely even discussed at all. Towards the beginning of our program, these young women were visibly uncomfortable when these questions were brought up. Many hesitated to even bring the questions up at all. I could see how self-conscious asking these completely valid and normal questions was making them feel.

My goal is to normalize these discussions that most young women long for, while providing every young woman the opportunity to learn these important life lessons and see that they are not alone. At the heart of all of these lessons, I want to encourage them to take a step back and consider the reasoning behind their actions - both internal and external - and take moments to pause, and reflect on why they do things or act in a particular way. I want these young women to see the importance of valuing themselves and not placing their value in the hands of others. Whether 'others' be friends, significant others, social media, or any other external source. I want them to be comforted by the fact that this is *their* book, *their* stories, *their* feelings, *their* journey.

I want to put your mind at ease and assure you that my goal is not to tell anyone what to think, how they should feel, or who they should be. Nor am I aiming to undermine any teaching, mentorship, or parenting preferences and lessons. I am simply wanting to provide these girls with a creative, mindful, and safe outlet for their reflection on their personal lives, how they view themselves, and how they can nurture their self-confidence and self-worth going forward - ideally taking this mindset of self-love and encouragement with them into their early adulthood and throughout their lives.

A BIT OF AN
INTRODUCTION...

Hey there! Before we begin, I want to let you in on a little secret...are you ready for it? You sure? Okay, here it is - I wrote
this book for you. It's true! And seeing that you and I are complete strangers, I have no reason to lie to you or mislead you.
The reasons that I decided to write this entire book all come
back to you. I guess this could seem kind of odd considering
that we don't really know each other. Heck, we don't actually
know each other at all. I am a total and complete stranger to
you, as are you to me. But I hope that by the time you finish
reading this book you will know a bit more about me - but
most importantly, you will learn a bit more about yourself.

My goal is to help you create confidence in yourself and to
help you to learn to love yourself. All while being totally open
and honest with you about the struggles and obstacles that I
had to overcome when I was in your shoes not so long ago. I
want to share with you the good, the bad, and the oh so ugly
that I experienced with the hope that it might help you to get
through whatever you're going through. So, here I am promising you...pinky promising even! That I will be completely honest with you throughout this entire book. That everything I
discuss with you is based on my personal experiences as a

young woman in my teenage prime, and what I wish I would have known then.

So...here I am sitting in my apartment wanting to share what I've learned in my life and what I wish I would have known while I was basking in my 'glory days'. Hard to believe it was a few years ago but trust me...It seems like yesterday. Ugh! Does using that expression make me sound like an old lady? Well I guess if I'm considered 'old' now, I prefer to go with the motto created by the one and only Beyoncé... *I'm a grown woman and can do whatever I want.* See - there are some perks to being 'old'.

Anyways, I remember my time as a young woman navigating the world of middle school, junior high, and high school and everything that came along with those years. And let me tell you (but of course you already know this) - it can be ROUGH!

I still remember the blissful memories, the days I wanted to last forever, the times I laughed until I cried, the butterflies, and the BFF's who I thought would truly be my best friends forever. I also remember the losses, the heartaches, the bad test grades, the gossip, the insane amounts of pressure, and the disappointments...I remember them all. Well, most of them anyways. And with all of those memories, I also remember the times it felt like I was the only one in the world who understood what I was going through. I remember walking through the hallways at school surrounded by my classmates, yet still feeling isolated, sad and alone. I remember the sheer terror of walking into the lunch room and realizing that you have no one to sit with. And I remember the nights where

I would fall asleep crying while thinking that things would never get better.

While you're going through these years of your life it seems like there are so many times when you think 'no one understands me' or 'no one knows what I'm going through'. And I want to let you know that there are people who understand what you're feeling. There are people who understand - or can at least try to relate - to what you're going through. Because we've all been there. You're not alone.

So I want to officially say to you and let you know that you are not alone. Did you hear me? YOU ARE NOT ALONE! Now one more time for the ladies in the back...YOU ARE NOT ALONE! I've been there. We've all been there. You're there now. And guess what...so are so many of the other girls in your squad, class, grade, school, etc. We've all been there at one time or another and it's important to know that you can and will get through it. Better yet...you'll get through it even stronger than you were going into it!

And I hope you get through it while continuing to love yourself, believing in yourself, and chasing whatever sets your soul on fire! You will get through it and come out stronger, prouder, and wiser. You will get through it with a sense of accomplishment and know that you can tackle anything and everything that comes your way.

So what does tackling your obstacles and challenges have to do with this book you're reading? And where might I have suddenly found the inspiration to write a book for the young women of today? Well, I found the inspiration in my little sister. And I am wanting to encourage you to tackle your obstacles and challenges, just as I want to encourage her.

So there is something you've now learned about me, I have a little sister...although she isn't so 'little' anymore and she would probably be embarrassed that I'm calling her my 'little sister'. Whatevs. Fine. Younger, I have a younger sister named Hallie. She's the bomb. I'm also really lucky because not only do I have a younger sister - but I have two younger cousins, Lily and Eleanor who are also awesome! All three of these young ladies are in the mix up of their adolescent, teenage years and all three of them are experiencing different joys and hardships in their lives.

While I did write this book for you, these three are my inspiration. Everything I do is with the hopes that they will see me as a positive role model in their life. Someone who will always be there for them, no matter what! And I hope that they see me as someone they can look up to - and that they hopefully *do* look up to. And that, my darling, is why I am writing to you. For you. I want to be here for you to help you get through this too.

So, whether you have ten siblings or two siblings, or if you're an only child. If you have twelve cousins, one cousin, or no cousins. If you have a dog who is your number one confidant, or a cat, or a goldfish (honestly, I prefer Beta fish to Goldfish but that's neither here nor there). What have you. I want to be there for you! I want you to feel heard and understood. I want you to know that you're not alone! I want to create a sense of community and belonging for those who are going through similar things to what you're going through right now. And lastly, I want to share my 100% honest, and real personal experiences and what I took away from my teenage prime with you. I'll share the good, the great, the bad, and the ugly with the hopes that you are able to take at least one small part of it with you. So, are you ready for this? Now that we're here...let's chat.

GIVE YOURSELF THE POWER
OF LOVING YOURSELF

Loving yourself, being yourself, and taking care of yourself gives you this amazing kind of power. And guess what...once you own that power, - no one can take it from you. Ever. Once you stop giving others the power to control the way you see yourself, what you think, and how you want to live your life, I promise you your world will start to change.

I think that the power of self is so important in fact, that if there is nothing else that you get out of this book, please learn that only you have the power and ability to make yourself happy. I mean truly, blissfully happy! Only you have the power to control how you see yourself. You have the power to control how you think about yourself. You have the power to control how you react in situations. You have the power to choose who you want to be in this world. You and only you have the power to feel confident in yourself, your abilities, the way you look, your goals, and your actions. You and only you have the power to control how you navigate these youthful years in your life. Don't let anyone take that power away from you. Seriously! This ability is so special and is something that we oftentimes don't think of as something that is within our control. And it totally is!

Brené Brown, a personal role model of mine, professor, lecturer, author, and podcast host, once said, "I now see how owning our story and loving ourselves through that process is the bravest thing that we will ever do." And I completely agree with her. Loving yourself and embracing the power of yourself is not easy! And it takes a lot of practice and patience with yourself. Heck, it's something that I am still working on, and I know that women of all ages across the world still have to choose to work on it each and every day. While I want you to be excited about how awesome the power of loving yourself is...I also want you to be gracious and patient with yourself as you work towards learning this power. Like all things in life - this takes practice. But I'm here to help guide you through it!

So think of me as your hype (wo)man! Of course, I want you to know that you're AWESOME! I want you to know how smart, kind, brave, courageous, beautiful, determined, and strong you are! I can think these things and tell them to you until I run out of breath. But it does absolutely nothing until you believe these things about yourself.

Wait...doesn't thinking all of these things about myself make me selfish? Self-centered? Conceded? Vain? HECK NO IT DOESN'T! It gives you power! It gives you peace, it gives you love, it gives you joy, it gives you the full permission and power to be you and own it! Isn't it so cool to think that there is not a single person who is exactly like you on this entire planet!? That you are the ONLY you in the entire world! It's honestly kind of crazy...you are the only you that ever has been or will ever be. Let that sink in. There has never been someone exactly like you, and there will never be someone exactly like you. Forever and all eternity. So why not be you! Yes...Kendrick says to be humble and I get that...but also get excited about the fact that you're you and that you're an original!

Are you starting to get excited? I'm pretty pumped just thinking about it. There's so much power in believing in yourself and controlling how you feel and see yourself. And I want you to believe that you deserve to feel as awesome as you truly are.

Chapter One Reflections

What are three things that make you feel awesome about yourself?

1.

2.

3.

What are three things that you wish you were more confident about?

1.

2.

3.

Why do you wish you felt more confident about these things?

How do you think feeling more confident about what you listed above will change how you feel overall?

POSITIVE THOUGHTS ARE LIKE
COLORFUL CONFETTI

What if I told you that it's all in your head..? Seems simple enough, huh? It's all in your head so let's just change the way you think! Boom-bam-done! Woahhh pump the breaks. Sorry to be the bear of bad news - but thinking positively can be really tough sometimes. Honestly, it is really hard to change the way you think about things. You know those moments when you have to focus and get in the 'zone'? Think of this chapter of learning how to get in the 'zone'. Think of it as the step in the right direction and embracing the art of recreating what you tell yourself.

The truth is, once we start looking at things differently it's crazy how the world seems to change right in front of our very eyes. Now of course let's not get *too* literal with this...I don't mean that if you look at an orange and think "turn into a pear" that it will somehow magically turn into a pear. What I mean is...that if you take a minute to slow down - pause - and take a step back and choose to look at a situation with a positive attitude, instead of taking on the feelings of worry, angst, and fret, that it might change how you see things! Heck, it might even change your attitude about whatever is unfolding right in front of you.

Okay, okay so thinking positively is supposed to change how I feel. It's supposed to change how I see myself and how I see the world around me. So how the heck do I do that!? Well...there are a lot of different ways, you have to figure out what works best for you! But remember - it takes patience with yourself and practice...lots of practice. Not what you wanted to hear...right?

What I have found is that the easiest way to work towards thinking positively is to look at things from a grateful, loving and understanding point of view. It's better to project love and support while working towards understanding, rather than looking at something and immediately thinking of the ways it falls short, could be different, better, etc. Let me try to better explain by using a few examples...

It's 7:00am on a Monday morning. Gross. You slept through your first and second alarm and are already starting the day off rushed and behind schedule. You get out of bed only to trip over your phone charger and stub your pinky toe on your night stand. OUCH! Oh, and to add to this mess - you just remembered that you forgot to complete your math homework from the night before. Great. Love it. You go into the bathroom to start to get ready and you're just not feeling it today. You hate the way your hair isn't cooperating, you don't like how your shirt is touching your stomach, you can't stand how your thighs look in your shorts, and ew what is that...? Another pimple?. Should I just change? What if Claire wears this shirt today too? Ugh then she'll be annoyed with me and I really don't want any drama right now. Speaking of drama...I wonder if I am going to have to see Ian in the hallway, he was such a jerk to me the other day I can't deal with this right now. Does this shirt make my arms look weird? Well should I wear my hair up or straighten it? Forget it...messy bun it is. Whatever. Great! It's not even 7:45am and my day already completely sucks. This day is ruined. Forever. For all eternity. Don't talk to me today.

UGH! Inhale, exhale, repeat! Because after reading that I feel stressed out! Don't you!? Isn't it crazy how just reading things and thinking in this negative self-talk can completely change your mood? I don't know about you, but while I was re-reading that, I felt my shoulders rise to my ears and my jaw started to tense up. I started to feel uncomfortable and insecure. I started questioning myself and honestly I started getting a bit annoyed. Which is crazy because in no way shape or form do I have any reason to feel this way. I'm not even close to being in this situation - It's 9:00pm and I'm sitting on my couch in my pajamas while Gossip Girl is playing in the background. Real talk, this is like the 5th time I have re-watched the series. I just can't help myself. Anyways, back to self-talk and positive thinking! Let's try to go through that same morning again but by applying some positive thoughts and a grateful, loving and understanding approach to self-talk.

It's 7:00am on a Monday morning. You slept through your first and second alarm. But hey, I'm up now and can totally work with the time I've got! I normally don't like Mondays but it was a great weekend! Let's have the goal to make this week an awesome week. I'm going to do great in class, I'll be super productive, and it's just going to be awesome. Ouch! Aw man I can't believe I just stubbed my toe...why does this always happen? And to my pinky toe too! Breatheeeee, it's all good. We're good. At least the thing didn't fall off or something. Crap, I totally forgot to finish those math problems that I wanted help with...Okay, okay, well I normally get to school a bit early anyways, so maybe I can work on it then! Or, while I'm eating breakfast or something. I'll figure it out. I could always ask Ms. Smith to help me and explain that I am having a hard time understanding what we're learning right now. Alright, into the bathroom we go. Let's get ready to slay the day. I love my eyes. Oh my bootay looks nice today too, heyyy. Dang girl, check you out. You are working those knots in your hair, let's just brush those out real quick. Thank you, body for being mine! Oh my gosh I love this top. Shoot, do you think Claire will wear hers today too? Well if she does we can be twinzzz lol. Honestly, what are the odds of that happening anyways. Oh gosh I completely forgot about that drama with Ian...breathe. No worries. If I see him then I will just smile politely and walk away. If I don't want to encourage his drama - then I am not giving him the satisfaction of lowering myself to his level. He doesn't get to control this situation - I do! It's my power. Remember - we're slaying the day today. Okay, I have all my things so Monday here we come!

Now how do you feel after reading that version compared to the negative self-talk version? So much better, right? I would even go as far to say that I felt a sense of peace after reading that. We so often let one little thing affect our entire attitude and then that tiny thing affects our whole day. It's kind of insane really. I get that sometimes it's easier to be negative. It's easier to be grumpy and have an attitude and blame the way you're feeling on exterior circumstances...but wouldn't you rather work to see the good in things? Wouldn't you rather see yourself with love? Wouldn't you rather work to understand others instead of fear their reactions? I promise you it's such a better way to live your life!

Let's take a little break to practice some positive self-talk. Repeat after me, out loud...seriously. Say these statements out loud to yourself.

- I am important
- I am loved
- I am kind
- I am smart
- I can do whatever I put my mind to
- I am brave
- I am courageous
- I deserve to be loved
- I deserve to feel happy
- I deserve great friends
- I am valued
- I am awesome

- I am the only me that has even been and ever will be. And that's really special.

Like I said...it isn't easy! And it's not to say that you won't have terrible days - because let's face it, bad things happen! It's a part of life. A crappy part...but a part nonetheless. And that's okay. My point here is to not get weighed down in all of the negativity. When you can, always try to lift yourself up with positive thoughts. Would you believe that at the age of 24 I am still working on having positive self-talk and trying to approach situations with gratitude, love and seeking understanding? It's true! And that's okay - because like I said - it takes practice! Positive thoughts and self-talk can not only help you with how you see/talk to yourself...but it can also help you to better navigate different events and situations that arise.

I was in a situation just last night actually where I caught myself practicing positive self-talk and trying to seek understanding. I was at a dinner for my job and one of my co-workers came up to me wanting to know why I 'hated Sam'. Let me add a disclaimer here...the co-worker who came up to me, Morgan, is new to our team, as is Sam. My personality is also a lot different from Sam and Morgan's personalities. I tend to be more quiet and introverted when I am not super comfortable around someone. So I believe Sam thought that my quietness meant that I must hate her - here is a moment where I had to pause - and try to seek understanding for where she might be coming from.

Continuing with the story now... Morgan continued to go on and on about how I must hate Sam and that Sam even told her the other day "I know Keri hates me." At first, I felt a bit attacked and defensive. I then remembered that I don't have to deal with this drama and I don't have to give it power or control over my emotions. I can choose to work on my own thoughts and not let this hiccup affect my happiness, thoughts, and the rest of the evening. I politely and directly responded to Morgan explaining that I am sorry Sam put her in such an uncomfortable situation, but I appreciated her letting me know her concerns. I explained that I would be happy to have a discussion with her about this later in private.

Unfortunately, Morgan wouldn't drop it and things were getting pretty uncomfortable. As I mentioned, this was a work dinner and there were several people around. She was getting upset and harshly threw out the comment 'well it's not like it's easy to fit in with this team'. Ouch...honestly, that comment hurt a bit. I couldn't believe she was bringing this concern up here and now, and that she was clearly so upset by it. Instead of reacting, I paused. I used my power of positive self-talk and had the following thoughts:

Keri...you don't have to react to this right now. This isn't a 'you' issue. Both Sam and Morgan are clearly insecure and are looking for ways to fit in. She is wanting to find her work squad, I get that. It can be hard. Morgan is clearly upset, I think her and Sam are becoming friends. They have been hanging out quite a bit. Her feelings are probably hurt by Sam's comment. After all, I know I would be protective of my friends too. Morgan is trying to find her work group too, she's probably just upset. Again, this isn't a 'me' issue.

I then smiled politely at Morgan and walked away. I took my power in that moment. I can honestly say that a few years ago, heck, even a few months ago I would not have had that calm of a reaction. I would have been livid! I probably would have verbally pushed back and would have become super defensive. But what good would that have done? It wouldn't have done any good. It would have created a scene and I only would have become more upset. Now, please know that you still have every right to stick up for yourself in these situations! What I'm saying is...before you react to a situation, pause, and ask yourself, is it worth it? Is this situation worth my reaction? Is this a 'me' issue, or a her/him issue? Then take a breath - pause - and then respond. Practicing positive self-talk is not easy. But it really does help...more importantly, it makes you feel better!

I know all of this info might have been a lot to take in, so let's recap - The power of self love involves your power. Your power to control how you feel, how you see yourself, how you react to situations, and what your thoughts are. Only you have the power to do this! We should try to use positive self-talk to reevaluate how we are looking at situations and circumstances. And while trying to look at these situations and circumstances from a place of gratitude, love and understanding - not judgement and negativity.

Remember, look with love, seek understanding, and pause to determine if it's a you issue or a him/her issue.

Chapter Two Reflections

What are five things that you love about yourself?

1.

2.

3.

4.

5.

How are you going to begin practicing ways of using positive self-talk?

What is a saying that you can tell yourself when you notice that you're thinking negatively?

FINDING BALANCE CAN FEEL LIKE YOU'RE WALKING ON A HIGH-DIVE BLINDFOLDED

I get it, girl - you've got A LOT going on. Between school, homework, grades, thinking about colleges, jobs, friends, romance, drama, siblings, parties, parents, finding yourself, etc. Your world always seems to be rapidly spiraling and spinning circles around you. Remember when you were younger and at recess you'd sit or lay down on the merry-go-round while your friends spun you as fast as they could? I would always get dizzy, sometimes a bit freaked out even! Heck, sometimes you were going so fast it felt like you could barely hold on!

Sometimes your life can feel like that too. It can feel like certain responsibilities are pulling you one way while other activities are stretching you in the completely opposite direction. It's exhausting, stressful, and a bit painful at times too. So how can you deal with that? How can you make it a little easier on yourself? How can you work to find *balance*?

To be real...having a healthy amount of balance considering all that you're involved in is really hard! And sometimes your balance can shift - after all, life isn't perfect. What matters is that you make working to find your balance a priority. And, that you're open and forgiving with yourself when your life starts to become unbalanced. When this happens, which it most certainly will at one point or another - you can take a moment to pause, reflect, and re-adjust how you need to move forward. Let me explain...

I'm in my twenties now and I am still trying to navigate how I can better balance my job, different schedules, my health, time for myself, my multiple hobbies, my friends, my boyfriend, and my family. It can be really tough sometimes! And while many of us desire to live a life that is perfectly balanced 100% of the time - I want you to know that this perfectly balanced life is not possible.

Remember when I promised you total honesty...well here's another example. As much as we might wish to live a fully balanced, stress free, organized life 100% of the time...there is no possible way that we can reach the point of balancing everything that we have going on all the time! Pleases don't let this scare you off though. Because while we might not be able to keep perfect balance in our lives 24/7, - we can always work towards making small improvements in our lives in which we feel more balanced. We can always work on trying to find ways to better organize our priorities, days, and time that we have available. Working on having a more balanced life is possible - having a balanced life 100% of the time is not. And that's okay.

I wanted to be honest with you and let you know that finding balance will probably be something that you have to work on throughout your entire life. And that's a good thing! Working to find your balance is so important. It can help you stay the course when unexpected things arise (which will happen). It can help you feel more at ease and organized about everything. It can help to lessen your sense of anxiety and panic when you're suddenly out of energy and time! And it can help you feel better about yourself. I truly think that the more organized you are, and the more open and honest you are with yourself about your priorities - the more at peace and in control you will feel in your day to day life.

On your journey to creating a more balanced life for yourself you will probably be faced with difficult decisions. Tough situations will arise where you have to prioritize everything that you have going on. You are going to be presented with different choices, opportunities, commitments, and difficulties. I personally believe that being active and involved in doing things is important, but I also believe that it is just as important to not do *too* much - especially if it's something that's not good for you.

After all, don't some of my main points for this book involve how you can get to better know yourself, how you can grow as an individual and learn to love yourself? YES! Yes they are. Thank you for remembering that, you rock. But how can you prioritize loving yourself and feeling good about yourself when you are exhausted and run down from all of the running around that you're doing!? The answer...you can't.

Please hear me say that finding balance and making these choices does not mean completely eliminating all stressful/ challenging/difficult situations. It does not mean that you can't do your homework. It does not mean that you can quit your commitments (in my opinion anyways...that might be a better discussion to have with your guardians or higher powers at be). It does not mean that you can ditch things or blow off your activities. What it does mean is that you should feel comfortable saying 'no' to an invite to a party this weekend if you aren't all that excited about - or if it isn't good for you to go right now.

Let's say that you really do want to go to that party, or hangout with your friends, or go to the lake this weekend - then to be able to do this, you have to balance what you are already committed to. So, if you already know all of the things that you have to get done this week before the party - then it is important to prioritize and have a game plan of when you are going to accomplish what.

Staying organized will bring you peace, it will make you feel better, it will help in school, in extracurricular activities, and I am sure Mom and Dad will appreciate it too. *Hello brownie points!* The point is, organization can be really helpful when you are striving to live a more balanced life. If you start practicing this now, it will be such a beneficial skill that you can continue to strengthen as you get older, I promise!

There are a few things that I find to be really helpful when it comes to trying to keep the balance in my life:

~ Meditation ~ Seriously! I love meditation. It is a great way to check-in with myself and see how I am feeling both physically and mentally. It is also a great break from the constant exposure to the stressful things that can pop up in life and on your feed. I am by no means a 'pro' when it comes to meditation, so I sometimes turn to different apps to help guide me through the meditation - remember, all good things take practice. Medication is also really simple and doesn't require much time! And you can pretty much do it anywhere! All you need is 30 seconds to 30 minutes to pause - mentally check-out (check-in with yourself) and give yourself permission to focus solely on you, your body, your feelings, and your thoughts.

Meditation Bonus - Stretching: I really enjoy stretching, weird right? Hear me out, at the end of the day, It's so nice just sitting on the floor and being able to unwind and focus more on my body and what it needs from me. I either stretch quietly or play some of my favorite songs. I look at this as taking a few moments to devote my time and energy to myself and my well-being. It's also really good for you, which is always a plus!

~ Highlighters, sticky notes, and cute planners galore ~ I am obsessed with planning out every aspect of my life. To be honest - I think I like it so much because it gives me the illusion that I have control. I think that if I plan out every aspect of my day then nothing other than these things can happen - in conclusion - I must have the ability to control everything that happens to me. Now you and I both know that this isn't true - but it's still really helpful to keep a planner to help you stay organized when you have so much going on! I also keep a planner. Because who doesn't love color coding things and fun pens? I also put things down in my work calendar on my phone. Whichever planning method works for you, use it and conquer it!

At the start of every week I write down all of the big things I have that week. Then I focus more on the day-to-day and the things I need to get done each day. This task takes anywhere from 10-15 minutes. 20 minutes if I am drawing cute flowers, squiggles, and doodles on the edges. I include everything in this planner: From when I am at work, to when I plan on devoting time to write, to work out, meditate, plans with friends, errands I need to run, etc. If I can plan out my day and see where I am devoting my time to, it really helps to keep me organized and on track. It also helps me to see if I have any 'free time' or 'wiggle room' in my day so I can better organize all of the things I need to accomplish.

Your planning might include items that are more like this: school, soccer practice, band practice, rehearsal, babysitting, Homecoming, work, dinner with grandma, little bro's baseball game, sleepover, Parker's birthday party, homework, working out, cleaning your room, studying for the Algebra test, chores, going to the movies, reading, hobbies, etc. Whatever it may be, if it is important to you, your education, and your goals, you should write it down and make sure that you are devoting your time and energy to it.

~ Self-expression ~ This is so important! Make sure that you are taking time to do things that bring you joy. For me, it's painting while listening to music, writing, or baking my incredibly delicious chocolate chip banana bread. Anything that allows you to take a breath and slow down - removing yourself from all of the craziness that is welcomed into your daily lives. Give some time to yourself, draw, sing, write plays, dream big, exercise, knit, what have you! If it makes you happy and brings you peace, it deserves to be a priority in your life.

~ It's okay to say "no, thank you" ~ For some reason, saying "no" or "no, thank you" always made me feel really bad. Like super guilty! How silly is that? I think it's because we, as girls, young women, women, etc., feel that it is important to devote time and energy to those we care about. And we care about others! We care so much that even sometimes it leads to sacrificing yourself and your best interests. Hear me out, it's wonderful that you are such a devoted friend! Your friends are really lucky to have you. But sometimes, if you've had a really long week, getting frozen yogurt with Becca can seem exhausting. Especially when you know that all she is going to want to do is gossip and talk about the mellow-drama that's taking over her life because of her recent breakup.

While it is important that you be there for your friends, it's also important that you take time to be there for yourself. So if you aren't pumped to hang out with Becca after school on Friday, kindly say that you can't, but you appreciate the offer. Maybe you could hang out next week or something? Whatever your response is, know that while you might feel guilty, please know that it is 1 million percent okay to make time for yourself! It doesn't make you a bad person, friend, sister, etc.

~ Checking in with yourself ~ With all of the things going on in the world, we easily sweep our needs to the side or under the rug. It's important to pause and reflect on things and really think about how you're doing. No really...how are *you* doing? Take a minute, do a few deep breaths, and ask yourself what you need. You can check in with yourself anywhere, really. In the car, in bed, while going to the bathroom, in between classes, anywhere. And it's important to do it often so you prioritize your feelings and assess how you're doing. I try to do this at least once a day.

Chapter Three Reflections

What are three things that you could be doing to give yourself more peace of mind and balance?

1.

2.

3.

What was something you could improve from this week to help you stay on track going forward?

What is your 'game plan' to have an awesome week next week?

How does organizing your week and activities make you feel? Why do you think you feel this way?

LET'S TALK ABOUT BODY IMAGE

How we see ourselves can either make or break our confidence. Trust me. It's so easy to focus on the things you don't like or to wish a certain part of you was different. While you work through this chapter, I really hope that you are able to start shifting your views and beliefs towards loving yourself. And as John Legend so tastefully sang, loving all 'your curves and all your edges. All your perfect imperfections'. Is it just me or is John Legend seriously like a gift to this planet? He totally is. You know it, I know it, Crissy knows it, case closed.

Body image definitely ties into positive self-talk and working towards loving yourself. Like I've mentioned in previous chapters - it can be really easy to think negatively about yourself. I personally think that we are our own biggest/worst critics. I know it's really easy to sit here and talk about body image and how you should work on changing the way you think. But I want to take it one step further to show you that I am in this with you! I want to take a deep dive and be open and honest with you to share one of my biggest insecurities with you. It's something that's bothered me since I was in middle school and to be honest some days I still struggle with it - even now. But I am working on it and I am working on continuing to love myself.

So, I did solemnly swear to be 100% honest with you, right? Right. I have always been incredibly insecure about my stomach. I'm not sure why...When I was growing up I would always try to cover my stomach by crossing my arms, or standing behind people or things. When I would try on clothes, I would make sure that they didn't really touch my stomach. I'd put on a new top and would immediately look at my stomach to make sure it was hitting in the right places. I'm being serious, I would IMMEDIATELY look at my stomach. No matter what. I couldn't even take a second to pause and see how the top fit me everywhere else. The absolute worst time was swimsuit season...I still feel so sad for my younger self and the hateful and anxiety ridden thoughts that I would tell myself and let myself believe. It didn't matter how cute my mis-matched suit from Target was (God bless Target, am I right?), I dreaded looking at myself in the fitting room. I dreaded trying on the suit only to see that my entire stomach was exposed. I hated it. Every second of it.

Then one of the biggest, most nerve-wracking moments of my life happened...the 8th grade graduation party. And to make matters worse...it was a pool party. I was so nervous! Not only did I have to wear a swimsuit in front of everyone, but in front of all of the boys! Also, I wasn't the most popular, prettiest, or skinniest girl in my grade. So in my mind that made matters even worse (we'll talk about the dangers of comparing yourself to others later). I completely ignored the fact that I was healthy, that my bikini was darling, and I was there to have a good time with my friends before we went on to high school! In case you were wondering...my bikini was a tasteful navy with cute little white, lace, flowers sewn into it. It was also scalloped on both the top and bottom. It was darling.

* * *

So, there we were at the 8th grade graduation party - I showed up in my t-shirt and Nike shorts with my bikini on under it, ready to go. I had even straightened my hair (which in hind-sight makes no sense considering it would be wet with pool water, but hey, I was looking good). We get there and start the evening off with pizza, games, ping-pong, etc. I was with my friends, getting to hang out with the guys, and everyone was really enjoying themselves. Then the time came where everyone was going swimming. I swear to you, as soon as I heard the announcement, I thought to myself "Oh holy crap. This is really happening. I was kind of hoping everyone just forgot about the whole 'pool party' thing." Nope. No one forgot about it. Super unfortunate.

Everyone starts to take off their coverups/t-shirts/etc. and heads into the pool area. I try my best to maintain a calm, cool, and collected composure. Inside I was low-key dying a slow and painful death. It's cool. no big deal. So there I am standing with my BFF, Rachel, and we are ready to enter the point of no return...we grab our towels, open the doors to the pool, and head in.

In my mind, everyone stopped what they were doing and looked at me. In my mind, they were all staring at all of my insecurities, saying to themselves 'Wow. Keri has a really weird stomach and such little boobs. I can't believe she even put a swimsuit on and thought that she could join us and fit right in. What a weirdo!' My negative self-talk was taking over.

But thankfully there was Reggie - one of my classmates. Reggie, came up and said hello, then asked us if we wanted to come play pool basketball with him and a few other guys. It's important to note here that Reggie was one of the most popular boys in our grade. He was smart, athletic, had a great smile, but above all...he was an incredibly nice, kind, and humble young man. Reggie would always go out of his way to make sure that everyone felt welcome and included. Looking back is probably what he was doing in this exact moment...I'm not always the best at hiding my emotions...especially when I am uncomfortable.

So, Rachel and I joined in the basketball game for a little bit. It was a lot of fun! After a while, we just wanted to hangout and catch up on all the latest gossip and all that was going on in our lives. On our way from the basketball area we stopped and claimed our little corner of the hot tub. Seemed like an appropriate place to sit and chat. So, there were talking about who had the cutest swimsuit, the classes we were planning on taking in high school, what we thought high school would be like, how cute the upper-classmen were going to be, and 'OMG when I turn 16 I can drive and finally have the total freedom I've been longing for since I was a small child'. Ahh the sweet naive-ness of our middle school selves...

In the middle of my explanation of what I thought my first car would be, I hear 'Dude. Move over we want in on this hot-tub action.' Ugh. Preston. Picture an annoying, conceded, and arrogant young man who thought he was more important than God himself. Anyways, in his bro-ey voice and his I'm-better-than-you attitude, he made it clear that we needed to make room for him and his bro-squad. So Rachel and I politely scooch over and made room. After all, it was a big hot tub so why not?

We tried to get back to chatting about how excited we were about the new, high school versions of ourselves, but it was incredibly hard to speak over the boys conversations of their Call of Duty plans this weekend, or how they *totally* are all going over to Chad's tonight because his parents were in Kansas City for the weekend for his sister's volleyball tournament. It was hard to continue our conversation between the loud and rowdy dude pool that had taken over our perfect hangout spot. Rachel and I decided that we were done swimming anyways, so we were going to get out and go play ping-pong or something - maybe then we could find some peace and quiet.

On our way out of the hot tub, I was chatting with my friend Christian. Just chatting and seeing how his night was going and if he was having fun. He was. I told him that Rachel and I were going to go play ping-pong and he could join later if he wanted to - It was then, that Preston ever so loudly claimed

"Hey, did you guys see Keri? She has such a weird stomach, am I right?". My entire world came screeching to a halt. Everything around me in that exact moment stopped. I thought that I died right then and there on the spot! Here it was, my worst fear playing out right in front of me. I was humiliated. I was shocked, I just stood there. I then see all of his friends turn and look at me, jaws dropped - they were in shock too. It was clear that Preston was completely unaware that I was standing right behind him.

Christian lightly kicked him on the shoulder, "Dude! Keri is freaking right here! Why would you say that!?" Preston turned in disbelief "Oh, s***. My bad Keri." I looked at him and then rushed over to Rachel so her and I could leave and go play ping-pong. I couldn't get out of there fast enough.

I kept pretty quiet about it. Rachel kept asking me if I was okay. I just acted like he was a stupid boy and I didn't let it bother me - when in reality, I was crushed. It was all I could do to not let myself cry. It was my worst nightmare coming true. I have never felt so small, unimportant, and insecure. Just talking about it here, now, in this book makes my heart hurt for my 14-year-old self. I didn't realize it then, but looking back I can so clearly see how this moment affected the way I saw myself for the next 10 + years of my life. Crazy, right? I gave all of my power to Preston and let it change the way I would look and feel about myself for the next 10 or so years!

Sure, my body didn't look like every other girls' in my class. But reality check! Your body doesn't look like anyone else's because it isn't supposed to! Your body was made for you.

Your body is your home. It's what is going to get you through your life, your struggles, your joys, and all of your journeys. So doesn't it only make sense that your body looks different from everyone else's because your body was made specifically for you and your life? It's custom made. Not one size fits all, or one size fits most. It's one size fits *you*.

I know now that Preston's comment is why when I try on clothes I immediately look at my stomach. I know now that it was this comment that made me sit a certain way, or suck in, or second-guess how I looked when getting ready for the future pool parties I would attend. But now I know that I should have NEVER let Preston's opinion dictate how I live my life or how I see myself! I wish I could say that I was able to come to this realization on my own - but I didn't. I had some inspiration from the book I recently read called *Girl, Wash Your Face* by Rachel Hollis. In the book, she explains that other people's opinion of you is none of your business. This could not be more true! (Side note: I highly recommend that you read her books when you are in your twenties. Her kind words, reliability, and words of motivation were the final push that I needed to start my journey on moving past this huge insecurity of mine - so Rachel, if you're reading this - Thank you!)

So what if Preston thinks I have a weird stomach? Why should his opinion keep me up at night? Why should his opinion keep me from wearing that swim suit that I love? Why should his opinion keep me from making the most out of moments instead of being so concerned about how I was sitting or how I looked?

The answer...IT SHOULDN'T! His opinion is none of my business. An important point that I also want to make here is that...do you honestly think that Preston even remembers saying those things about me? I honestly doubt it. Yet, I've lived a big part of my life letting this one little comment, this little opinion, dictate my life choices, behavior, and a large portion of how I felt about myself.

So, here I am talking to you wanting you to hear about a very personal and vulnerable moment that happened in my own life and what I took away from it some 10 years later. I want you to know that other people's opinions of you should not dictate how you live your life. Even more, I want you to know that you have the power to control what you do and do not believe. If people have mean, hurtful, opinions of you. That's just that...they are their opinions and should have no power over you and the way you see yourself. Do you hear me? It's very important so I am going to say it one more time...People's opinions are their opinions and should have no power over you and the way you see yourself.

You get to control what you think, how you feel about yourself, and how you react to the opinions that come in and out of your life. Trust me, opinions are like belly buttons...everybody has one. So it's up to you to choose whose opinions you let affect you, and whose you simply let pass you by.

Chapter Four Reflections

Can you think of a time when someone said something about the way you looked that hurt your feelings? I want you to think about that for a second and then respond to the questions below...

What did they say to you or about you?

How did that make you feel?

Has that moment changed the way you see yourself, what you wear, or how you act? In what ways?

What do you think would have changed in your life, if you let this opinion/statement not have power over you and the way you see yourself?

Going forward, how can you remind yourself that people's opinions of you are none of your business?

What about your body is special? What are the things that are unique about your body that make it the perfect size/body for you?

FOLLOW, TWEET, SNAP, DM, LIKE, ETC. - APPROVE ME

Here it is, the chapter on social media and the dangers that come with it...blah, blah blah. I'm sure you're expecting me to say how dangerous social media is, or how you are 'addicted to it' or 'back in my day...'. Alright, cool it. That's not what this chapter is about. Let's just go into it with an open mind and try to look at social media from a different point of view, deal?

From middle school onward I have seen the significant growth of the role that social media plays in our lives. I've seen how it has both positive and negative effects! While yes, I believe that there are quite a few negatives to it - I also see a lot of cool things about it. I think it's great that you have a platform to express your thoughts, insight, beliefs, and your feelings. I think it's great that social media provides you with an outlet to creatively express yourself and who you are as a young woman. I really do! But as you read this chapter, I want you to take a few different things into account about the ways we view and use social media. So again, all I ask is that you try to look at the use of social media with an open mind.

My plan here is to shed a bit of light on some things that come along with the use of social media - and some things that I want you to really pay attention to, okay? So let's work through this topic together, because I have learned that some of you have pretty fierce opinions on social media use and its purpose in your day-to-day world. So, let's talk about it! Take a look at the questions below and let me know your answers. There are no wrong answers here.

What do you think is great about social media?

1. _____
2. _____
3. _____
4. _____
5. _____

What do you think is not so great about social media?

1. _____
2. _____
3. _____
4. _____
5. _____

Like I said earlier, I think that there are a lot of great things about social media! However, I alsobelieve that there are some not so good things. The first, being that sometimes social me-

dia creates a lot of unnecessary stress and can place importance on things that aren't necessarily that important...

How many followers do you have on your Instagram or Fin-
sta account? How about your Snap score? Who is on your best
friend list? Do you know these numbers/stats right off of the
top of your head? If so - or if you had a pretty close guess - why
do you think these numbers came to you so quickly? Why
are these numbers important to you? You see, in my experiences with talking to young women about their social media
accounts, they often think that the more followers you have,
the more important/popular/prettier/cooler you are.

Let's not forget about the follower to following ratio! I'm
sorry...what? So if we were really to dig deep into this logic,
then we would be saying that you have a limit to who you
can follow based on the amount of people that follow you...?
Seems kind of odd, right? I mean, you're telling me that I can't
follow another account that posts pics of the world's most
adorable puppies since I don't have enough followers to bridge
the gap?

The amount of limitations and restrictions that must take
place to keep the ratio correct must be exhausting - and let's
be completely honest - what will really happen if you don't
have the perfect follower to following ratio? Will the Earth
suddenly stop rotating around the sun? No, it won't... My point
here is that I know these things seem so important, but can
you see how they might not really be *that* important? And that
they shouldn't be so important that they have an effect on

how you see yourself or how you should go about living your life.

The amount of people that follow you is seen as your status. Meaning that if you have more than 2,000 followers you must be the coolest, most popular and prettiest girl in your class/school/city. If you have more than 1,000 + followers you're like in second place from the girl who has 2,000 followers. You're still really pretty and pretty popular, but there is still room for improvement (more followers). If you have more than 500 followers you're alright I guess but are either really particular about who you let follow you or you aren't nearly as cool as the chick with 1,000 or 2,000 followers. - Doesn't this seem so harsh when we speak about it like this? Seriously, please know that I don't believe these things at all! In fact, to be brutally honest with you, I don't care how many followers you have - it doesn't matter to me.

How could I not care about how many followers you have!? I must not get it. Since I am older than you, I must not understand how important social media is and the major role it plays in your life. Here I claim to be your biggest supporter, your hype (wo)man, yet I don't care about the amount of work, filters, or hunts for perfect lighting that you've made to achieve your exact number of followers. How dare I!?

I promised you honesty, so here it goes... I don't care about the amount of followers you have. I don't care, because the number of followers that you have does not mean that you are more or less important or valued. Does this make sense? I know that it seems like having a ton of followers makes you more important, but it doesn't. It really doesn't. Here, humor me and think of it this way for a second...

Does having more followers mean that you're a good person? Does having more followers mean that you are loyal to your family and friends? Does having more followers mean that you are a hard worker and dedicated to your studies? Does having more followers mean that you're a loving person and that you love yourself? Does having more followers mean that you follow your dreams and fight for what's right? Does having more followers mean that you are fulfilled with yourself and what your goals for your future are? Does having more followers mean that you see yourself differently when it's just you and the mirror?

No, no and nope. Having more followers does not measure ANY of these things! You are not a number. You are not the amount of followers that you do or do not have! This number does not determine if you're a good person, it does not determine if you are loved or if you love yourself and it certainly doesn't determine your happiness. I know that after you finish this chapter, heck, this book even, that you will still go about your lives and that social media will more than likely continue to play a major role in your life. Which is fine.

All that I am asking - all that I am hoping for - is that the next time you drop from 200 followers to 199 followers that you take a second to remember that it is not because of you, nor does that drop in followers determine how significant you are. I want you to remember that this really doesn't matter and this won't affect the fact that you love yourself and that you're awesome. Can you promise me that?

Anytime you are looking at your account and starting to place the value and importance on yourself and the amount of followers that you do or do not have, remember that we had this discussion and your happiness, worth, sense of self-love and value do not come from your social media accounts.

❚ You are worthy. You are valued. And you are loved. Period. ❚

The second topic related to social media that I would like to chat about would be how social media can make you feel. Seems kind of silly, huh? How could social media change the way I *feel*? Lemme tell ya girl, it definitely can.

One thing that is great about social media is the fact that it allows for you to stay in touch with your friends and keeps you in the loop with what everyone is up to. With everything going on in your world (remember the section that talked about finding balance?) it can be hard to keep in touch with everyone! But think about this for a second...do you really *need* to stay in touch with everyone 24/7? Is this really that great of a thing to do?

Sure, the snap streaks are great, but when you snap one another constantly are you even talking to each other? Or is it just some photo of half your face while you're looking into the distance trying to be nonchalant about your level of involvement (or lack thereof) with that snap? All to increase your snap score? I do have a question for you that I am truly curious about...does talking to each other all the time take away the specialness of seeing one another at school or practice the following day? I ask this because every time, well most days, when I would see my friends at school we would be pumped to tell one another what happened while we were at home. Whether my brother got grounded, or what Rachel's dad said at the dinner table that made her really embarrassed, or any other detail about our evening that we felt was relevant and important for our friends to know.

I feel like "talking" to one another constantly and out of obligation would take this experience away and make seeing each other all the time less real, special...does it?

Recently, I took a 40 day break from all of my social media accounts. Facebook, Snapchat, Instagram, TikTok, Pinterest, all of it. Why would I do such a thing, you ask? I started noticing changes in how I was feeling...I started to feel a bit 'on edge' and more anxious than usual. I feel that it's important to note here that I have struggled with diagnosed anxiety for a majority of my life and that being anxious has become a normal part of my everyday life. However, I was noticing that it had increased even more than it usually was.

I would find myself mindlessly clicking on these apps on my phone when I really didn't even want to look at my accounts, or really without even thinking about it. I also noticed that I was comparing myself to the young women that I would see on my feed. It would start to make me feel bad about myself and the way I looked, or more specifically, because I didn't look a certain way.

I know that I've talked to you about the importance of positive self-talk and loving yourself as the way you are, but that (for me anyways) is a life-long goal. It's something that I have to work on daily and it is a constant decision that I make to try and choose to love myself. It's hard, but because of my practicing I know that I am valued, loved, and worth it. So back to my social media cleanse...

I'd find myself mindlessly scrolling through my feeds without even reading or paying attention to what I was looking at. I wasn't even using these apps, really, yet they were taking up almost all of my free time! Crazy! When I noticed these changes, I thought to myself...maybe I can give these up. Maybe if I don't use social media for the next 40 days then I can lessen my anxiety a bit, not feel as 'on edge' and can make better use of my time. And that's exactly what I did.

It was *really* tough at first. I would find myself pulling out my phone and wanting to immediately and mindlessly scroll through these accounts...but ha.ha. Thankfully I was smart enough to know that I would do this, so I deleted them from my phone completely. So when I would do this, I'd be reminded 'oh yeah, I don't have social media right now...now what?'

It felt awkward just sitting there without my tiny shield from the world around me. What am I supposed to do? Where do I look? Crap I just made really awkward eye contact with those people. What do I do with my hands? I'll leave them on my lap, that seems normal. Hello, self. What are your thoughts today?

I swear to you, not scrolling through my phone felt like I was learning how to swim or ride a bike for the first time. Uncomfortable and unpleasant. But then...I started to see subtle, but important changes in myself and my day to day life. First off, I was sleeping so much better! I also started to notice little things around me, like the new flowers in the garden of our apartment building, or the smell of the freshly baked pastries from the French café on the corner. I'd look at what people were wearing and how they were expressing themselves through style. I saw all sorts of 'new' things in my world that I had been closed off to before!

Pretty soon, it became my new normal! I'd come home from work and instead of pinning my dream wedding ideas, or cakes that I will probably never make, I read books that I had been wanting to read for years. I painted while listening to my favorite songs, or I'd meditate more, or I'd go on walks. I began to do so many things that truly brought me joy. And in doing these things, I felt like I was just starting to really live my life again! It was so refreshing. I see how this might seem kind of weird, and over the top - I mean aren't we always living our lives? What I mean is, I felt like I was making my life come to life, that I was engaging in my day-to-day world and taking part in my reality. It's a great feeling! It actually made me feel like I was in the present. Like I was finally living my life.

* * *

So here we are today and some time has passed since I gave up social media for 40 days. At first it seemed weird using it again. Almost boring even. But I am back to using it now - but not as much. I'll hop on my account to see what's going on and how my family is doing, and then I hop off and continue reading, or even writing. I understand that it seems crazy to ask you to give up social media, so I'm not going to do that. What I am going to ask of you though is that you start using mindfulness when you are using social media.

What does mindfulness look like? Well I am glad you asked! Mindfulness is when you take control over a moment by being present and bringing awareness to your thoughts, feelings, surroundings, body, and environment through a gentle and loving perspective. When we take on the form of mindfulness, we are looking at our thoughts and sensing what is happening in the current moment, rather than letting our minds wonder and worry about the past, future, or other things.

So how would I use mindfulness when using social media? Another great question! When you're looking through your feed, are you actually looking? Or are you mindlessly scrolling? When looking at images of other young women, do you feel happy for them, or do you immediately start to compare yourself, the way you look, or your lifestyle to theirs? When you see a group of friends hanging out without you, do you feel hurt and upset, or genuinely happy for them? If you see a beautiful sunset, do you HAVE to snap it to show everyone? Or do you feel like you can sit back and take in its beauty?

It's all about taking a step back to pause and check-in with yourself to see how you're feeling. So, to be clear - I am not asking you to give up social media. I am just suggesting that when you're using it in your day-to-day life, remember to pause and see how it's affecting you. And, if you decide that a little break might be beneficial for you, then go for it!

Chapter Five Reflections

Why do you feel that social media is important to you?

1.

2.

3.

4.

5.

Give some examples of times when social media has made you feel good about yourself.

1.

2.

3.

Give some examples of times when social media has made you feel bad about yourself.

1.

2.

3.

What are some ways you can work towards being more mindful while you're using social media?

Would you ever take a break/cleanse from social media? Why or why not?

REFLECTIONS CAN BE DECEIVING - LIKE THOSE DISTORTED MIRRORS AT THE CARNIVAL

Woop Woop! Chapter 6! You're putting quite the dent in this book, way to go! So we've talked about the power you have, we've talked about positive thoughts and finding balance, we've also looked at body image and social media...that's quite a bit and there's still more to go. Now, I'd like to have you look at society's standards of beauty and what that means for you, as well as the dangers that comparison can bring. See, I told you we'd talk about this later! Here we are!

Let's start with society's standards of beauty. In college, I did a lot of research on how women are represented in the beauty and fashion industries and how this representation can affect our self-esteem. After hundreds of hours spent on research, numerous papers, and several in-dept class discussions and debates, I've concluded that the most important thing to remember when you see models, runway shows, or magazines is that it is an empire-like industry that employs those who fit into the industries standards. Okay, so what do I mean by this statement? After all it seems like a pretty simple, generic statement for a multi-billion-dollar industry.

Think of famous athletes...What do they look like? If you picture a basketball player - she is probably pretty tall (depending on her position), has toned, muscular arms, is solid and is built like a basketball player. How does a soccer player look? She probably has killer legs, is toned, healthy and looks like a soccer player. How does a gymnast look? She probably is on the shorter side but is ripped and incredibly strong - she looks like a gymnast. You can go on and on for every sport, but the point is that these athletes look and represent the sports that they play - they represent their industry. They look this way because it is their job to be fit, strong, healthy, and athletic. It is their job to be a famous basketball player, soccer player, gymnast, etc. They have to look the part to do their job.

The same applies for models. It is their job to either maintain their thin figure or plus sized figure. It is their job to look a certain way, wear their hair a certain way, have their makeup applied a certain way, wear certain clothes, eat certain foods, etc. It is their JOB to do this. They are literally getting paid to workout, stick to a certain diet, and maintain a certain regimen and look a certain look that is only achievable if they keep living the way they are living and doing their job. Therefore, you CANNOT compare yourself to the way a woman looks in a magazine. You can't compare yourself to a Victoria Secret or PINK model, you can't compare yourself to the Instagram influencers, you just can't. Why? Because it isn't your job to look/dress/or act a certain way. It isn't your job to look like them.

For those of you who aspire to be a model when you grow up - go for it! You do you. And please know that I am in no way trying to deter you from pursuing your dream. What I am saying is that now, at this time in your life...your job is to get an education and go to school. Your job is to do your best in the extracurriculars you are involved in, if you are employed then your job is to show up to work on time and be a good employee, your job is to lay a healthy foundation of self-love for your future self in the years to come. This is your job, not looking like the woman on the cover of a magazine.

This leads up to our next topic of comparison and how important it is to not compare yourselves to others. I know we've touched on it a few times, but I feel that it's so important that we should touch on it again. Just like you shouldn't compare yourselves to models, you shouldn't compare yourself to your friends, sister, cousins, classmates, etc. Remember earlier how I said that your body is one-size-fits-you? If you don't remember it, then go back to that section because it's important.

You shouldn't compare the way you look, what you have, or where you are at in your life to how others look or what others have or are doing in their lives. Have you ever looked around and noticed how different we are from one another? Not comparing, but just observing how truly different we all are? Some of us have long legs, others short. Some of us have blonde hair, some red or black, some of us have freckles, others don't, and so on and so forth. We are all very different and it's really cool! So instead of comparing ourselves to one another, why not embrace what makes us different!?

I know this can be really hard to do. My best friend growing up – remember Rachel? – had beautiful, full, voluptuous, wavy, long, blonde hair. I loved the way it looked and desperately wished that my hair looked like that. My hair, on the other hand, is very fine, straight, and brown. Growing up I didn't like it at all because I felt it looked like string beans hanging off of my head or hair that belonged to a mouse. I was constantly comparing my hair to other girls and was always cutting/dying/styling it any way that I could to make it look different. It honestly wasn't until about 2 years ago that I started to miss my natural hair color and style, so I stopped dying it and am letting it grow out all natural now. I love my hair now.

The point is, back then I loved Rachel's hair. I would constantly compare my hair to hers and it obviously was never going to look like that, so it made me feel crummy every time I would try and change it and it didn't end up looking exactly like hers. The funny part is, Rachel hated her hair! She absolutely hated it. For her, it was too curly and messy and took forever to straighten. She could never wear it a certain way that she wanted and thought that it was the worst.

So here I am comparing myself to her, wishing I looked more like her, and she hated the way she looked. Seems like a never-ending cycle, huh? I think that we always wish something was different. Whether we always compare ourselves to others while wishing our legs were more like hers, or that our hair could look like that in a messy bun, or that my eyes were like hers, the list goes on and on.

But wouldn't it feel so much better if instead of trying to change ourselves to look more like someone else, if we instead started loving the way that we each look? Can you imagine how you would feel at a pool party if you walked in and felt confident and in love with your body and the way you are instead of comparing yourself to every other girl there? It doesn't just have to be a pool party; can you imagine living your life this way!? Imagine the giant weight that would be lifted off of your shoulders if you were able to go throughout life feeling fully confident in who you are.

This is something that is really hard to learn. I am 24 now and have really just started to become confident in myself and who I am as a young woman, which is great! But my late start to this also sometimes saddens me. I'll look back at old photos and think to myself "why couldn't I see how cute I looked in that top?" or "I wish I was happier there. I remember how nervous and uncertain I felt and it was awful." There are still times when I catch myself making comparisons. But now when I do this...I pause and make a friendly reminder to myself that I am beautiful the way I am. Instead of comparing - I try to say to myself, "Good for her. She's awesome and I wish her happiness. I love myself just the way I am. And I am awesome."

So, I share this with you in the hopes that you will be able to get a better head start than I did. I share this with you, so you can stop imagining and start working on becoming more confident in yourself, who you are as a young woman, and your abilities. You are a treasure and it's important that you know that.

Chapter Six Reflections

How are you going to work on not comparing yourself to other girls?

What are you going to say to yourself when you catch yourself making comparisons?

What are things that you can do to make you feel good about yourself, who you are as a person, and how you look?

How is the way you look perfect for you and your life?

CAN I HAVE A PUMPKIN SPICE LATTE WITH A SPLASH OF GRATITUDE, PLEASE?

Not going to lie, I would be incredibly grateful for a PSL right about now...but it's currently July, so that's unfortunate. Okay, obviously practicing gratitude is much more than being grateful for our favorite Starbucks drink. Gratitude is about taking a moment to pause and be grateful for all that is going on around you and for all that is good in your life. More specifically, gratitude teaches us to have a greater appreciation of circumstances or things and express this sense of appreciation with grace and kindness.

Practicing gratitude can benefit our lives in so many ways! Seriously, it's actually pretty cool. Practicing gratitude can make us happier, less stressed, and can even strengthen our emotions and relationship with self. There are a lot of benefits to doing something that is so simple! Gratitude isn't this hippy dippy peace, love, feeling some magical energy or anything.

It's just a great way to check-in with your thoughts and where you are at right now and remind you of all that is good around you.

Another great thing about gratitude is that it can apply to anything! You can be grateful for the shoes on your feet, to your dog, to the coco puffs you had for breakfast this morning. When I practice gratitude, I like to split it into two categories. I call it little picture and big picture gratitude.

I do this because there are so many things that I am grateful for, that it's often hard to choose a select number (I usually choose three of each). I found that if I limit myself to three total, and not doing the 'big' and 'little' picture gratitude - then I usually focus on more 'big picture' things like my family, job, breathing, my apartment, boyfriend, etc. By no means am I saying that these things aren't important! I'm just saying that sometimes it's nice to focus on the 'little picture' things like my new pair of leggings, the delicious coffee that I had this morning, the nice waitress at the restaurant where I had lunch, my new phone case, fuzzy socks, or my newest book. Things like that.

I think that focusing on both the big picture and little picture things can help put things into perspective and shows me how blessed I really am. And how thankful I am for everything and everyone in my life. At first, practicing gratitude felt foreign to me. I wasn't sure what the 'right' things were that I should be thankful for and I wanted to make sure that I wasn't being basic and snobby for being grateful for materialistic items like leggings. But you know what...I am grateful for my leggings. And that's okay, because this is my practice of gratitude and I can be grateful for anything and everything that I want.

So, let's brainstorm a bit...what are some 'big picture' things that you can be grateful for? Well, you could be grateful for your home because it keeps you and your family safe and comfortable. You could be grateful for your family because you love them and they are important to you. You could be grateful for your friends because they're always there for you. You could be grateful for your school and education because so many people across the world aren't able to get an education. You could be grateful for your health. You could be grateful for your teachers or mentors. You could be grateful for a recent vacation, or an experience, etc. Anything really!

How about 'little picture' things? To me, little picture gratitude includes being thankful for my new leggings because they are super comfortable and I feel good about myself when I wear them, or my new coffee maker because it saves me 10 minutes every morning, or my new phone case because I love the flowers on it, or the walk I took earlier this afternoon because it was nice to get outside and clear my head, or my new pillow because it's super squishy. It can be anything that you wouldn't classify as important as 'big picture' things, but still makes you smile and is something you are thankful and grateful to have. Make sense?

I practice gratitude every night while I am laying in bed. You could do it in the morning or throughout the day. I just prefer to do it at night, so I can reflect on everything that happened during the day. While I am lying there, I take a deep breath - then I begin reflecting on my three big picture things - followed by my three little picture things that I am grateful for. At first it will seem strange, maybe even kind of silly...But if you keep at it and keep practicing then it will start to feel normal. It will start to be relaxing for you. And it will start to help you feel better about yourself and all that is good in your life.

Chapter Seven Reflections

What are three big picture things that you are grateful for?

1.

2.

3.

What are three little picture things that you are grateful for?

1.

2.

3.

When do you plan on practicing gratitude each day?

Do you think practicing gratitude will help you?
Why or why not?

HEALTHY HABITS...AND SOME THIN MINTS

One of the things that I wish I would have been better about during my teenage years was developing healthy habits and taking the time to take care of both my mental and physical health. While I was in shape during the whatever sports season was taking place (soccer, track, volleyball, or basketball), I didn't necessarily continue the habit of working out into the off season. I didn't think that it was important, and I knew that the next season would come around soon enough. I also didn't think about the importance of fueling my body through the food I was eating. Nutrition really wasn't a 'thing' in my mind...

Working out isn't just about trying to look good - working out and being active is such a great way to boost your confidence, refresh your mind, and feel good about yourself! It also keeps you healthy! When I would workout in my teenage years it was all about training my body for whichever season I was in. If it was soccer season, I would work to become more toned, leaner, and gain the ability to run for a while, while still being able to sprint if needed. During track season I would work on building my endurance, while strengthening my abs and calfs to help me succeed at high jump. If it was volley-ball season, I was perfecting my vertical, gaining arm muscle, and making sure that I could dive on the floor and pop back up without missing a beat. If it was basketball season, it was all about bulking up and gaining muscle mass while still being able to sprint up and down the court.

Sitting here thinking about all these different fitness regi-mens is actually kind of crazy. I'm sure my teenage body was probably like "Hey, lady! What the heck are you doing to me!? Just make up your mind!" This kind of training is of course a part of being an athlete, I knew that then and I know that now. But what I would like to focus on now is finding that sweet spot with your body's health while also being able to maintain a solid fitness routine. Even if you aren't an athlete! It doesn't matter! Finding a time and regimen that works for you too is just as important. Even if it's just 15 - 30 minutes a day, get-ting up and moving is incredibly important. It is a great way to wake your body up and boost your creative juices and energy levels. You don't have to do anything crazy or have a strict rou-tine that you stick to. Just doing something active every day - from walks to runs to lifting to dancing. Different activities will help keep you healthy and will lay the groundwork for the years to come.

It's important to take care of our bodies and develop these healthy habits sooner, rather than later. Trust me, you'll thank me when you're graduating college and have set the tone for what your body expects of you when it comes to getting in some active movement every day. You'll hopefully be thankful for these habits all the way into your twenties, and onward in your life as well.

Nourishing your body and making sure that you're eating well is also really important! Looking back, I can remember several occasions where I would come home from school and eat an entire pack of Chips Ahoy Chocolate Chip Cookies. Seriously...the entire pack. And I'd wash them down with some chocolate milk. I am by no means telling you to diet, count calories, or strictly watch what you eat, all I am saying is that it's great to be mindful about what you're eating.

Make sure that between the pizza, Goldish, and Sour Patch Kids that there is some fruit, veggies, or a salad thrown in there. Make sure that between the Gatorade, Dr. Pepper, and Peach Tea that there's a nice, hydrating, glass of ice water or two. Remember, we're striving to love ourselves and taking care of our bodies because we deserve that. You deserve that.

I don't want you to think of mindful eating and the importance of nutrition as a bad thing. Don't think of it as limitations or rules - instead, try to switch your mindset to see that having proper nutrition is a good, powerful thing. Think of it as the fuel for your body - think of it as a great honor of self care. You're caring about what you're putting into your body. You're choosing to eat good things because you deserve to feel good and be healthy.

But with this new healthy mindset - I also want to reiterate again, it's 100% okay to still enjoy brownies, ice cream, and slushies! Heck, I still struggle with self-control when it comes to Girl Scout Thin Mint Cookies. Again, here I am mindlessly pounding one sleeve in 30 minutes. But like I said - this is a journey and it takes practice! I'm still practicing this too. My point here is, that if I would have been more mindful about what I ate during my youth, it might have made it easier for me in my twenties to have healthier eating habits. So your journey on this can start now!

Chapter Eight Reflections

What do you currently do to be healthy and active?

What can you start doing to increase how active you are?

Why do you think it is important to take care of your body and health?

How do you plan to introduce healthier foods into your daily meals?

YOU ARE MORE THAN YOUR
POSSESSIONS

I remember walking into the girls locker room before my 5th period gym class. I also remember how annoyed I was that my gym class was scheduled during 5th period - which meant I would be smelly, sweaty, and gross for the remainder of the day - But I was so excited because I had recently gotten a brand new pair of tennis shoes from my grandma for my back to school gift. I couldn't wait to put them on! I had been wanting this pair of shoes for months...They were KangaRoos (look 'em up if you're curious - they were pretty sweet). And mine were the coolest! The souls were white, and the main body of the shoe was light green. The Kangaroo itself was a teal blue, to match the teal blue laces, and I believe the inside of the shoe was purple. They were so cool and I couldn't wait to wear them.

As I was getting dressed for gym class, I noticed that all of the other girls were putting on their gym shoes. A lot of them had new Nike Shocks that they must have gotten during their 'back to school' shopping. They looked awesome! All the neon colors, and the jelly shocks making each girl about an inch or two taller. I started to doubt how cool my shoes were...But I had just been so excited about my new shoes. Why wasn't I as excited anymore? Why was the fact that the other girls had Nike Shocks and I chose my KangaRoos bothering me? I thought Nike Shocks were cool...but I didn't really want a pair. I wanted my KangaRoos - so why did I suddenly care about what everyone else was wearing and the fact that I didn't have the same thing they did?

I remember looking back down at my feet and telling myself "...but I really like my shoes. Why do I suddenly want a pair of Nike Shocks?" I know now that I was placing my value and coolness ranking, or being 'popular' in my possessions. I was placing my value in my new shoes. Knowing what I know now I wish I would have had the confidence to not care about what the other girls were wearing. I wish the fact that I loved my shoes would have been enough. But there was some underlying desire to keep up and fit in with my classmates. This is a feeling that adults have too! It's such a common feeling that they even made an expression for it - "Keeping up with the Joneses".

The feelings I was experiencing were based on my thought process of "If I have a pair of Nike Shocks...then I'll be cool like Jessie." Now this of course isn't true. And it's a really hard thing to realize when you're in the moment during these kinds of situations. Now hear me out - say your classmate, Becca, has a really cool pair of leggings. They're like super cute and you love the color, style, and how they look! You honestly just love the leggings...then if you have the means, go get the leggins, girl! But - what I don't want you to do is see Becca in her leggings and see that she has the 'perfect body', that she's popular and everyone loves her, and that she has long sun-kissed hair...and if you get those leggings then you'll have all of that too! No. you won't. And you don't need to!

It doesn't matter what shoes you're wearing, or if your leggings are the coolest, new leggings from the hottest brand. It doesn't matter that all of the other girls are wearing Air Force Ones, but you love your Converse. Wear the Converse! You need to wear the things that make you happy - not things that you think will make you prettier, cooler, or more popular. Work on being comfortable in your own skin. In your own clothes. And work on being comfortable with who you are as a person and loving yourself!

Please know that this doesn't happen overnight...remember, this is going to take practice. Loving yourself, and accepting who you are on the inside and the outside, is something that you will have to work at for the rest of your life. Heck, I'm still working at it too, remember? But it's a daily choice that we all get to make when we wake up in the morning - I'm going to put on my cool new leggings with pockets because I love pockets! I'll wear my favorite t-shirt because it's super soft and has an adorable design on it...and I'll put on my Kanga-Roos because I am obsessed with these shoes and they make *me* happy. Do what makes *you* happy.

Chapter Nine Reflections

Have you ever compared what you were wearing to what
someone else was wearing? Write down what happened and
how it made you feel.

Is there a girl in your class/grade who you wish you could dress
like? Do you wish that because she has great fashion sense - or
because you wish you were here? It's okay to be honest...

If you answered 'you wish you were her' above...why do you
wish that? There's no judgement here.

Think about 5 things that make you unique and special - Maybe they are qualities that no one else has - what are they?

1.

2.

3.

4.

5.

What are 3 possessions/items that you have that you LOVE? Why are they so special to you?

1.

2.

3.

FRIENDSHIPS AND RELATIONSHIPS HAVE 'GOOD' AND 'BAD' DAYS TOO...

The bond you create with your friends can be such an amazing and meaningful connection. Friends are like extensions of us - in a way - they're people we identify with, people we choose to spend our time with, people we love to hangout with, people who make us laugh, who encourage us to do our best and show their continued support through it all. Friends are the people who are there for us no matter what. There the ones we can tell our deepest, darkest secrets to. Friends 'get it'. They know you better than anyone and are the people that you can talk to about anything! They're the ones who you want to hangout with and grow up with! Aren't friends the best!?

At least...they're supposed to be...but that doesn't always happen. And, it's important to know that that's okay. Sometimes we try so hard to become friends with someone, or to fit into a certain friend group, that we forget to pause and ask ourselves - do I even really like these people? Are these 'good people'? Do they believe in me and what I believe in? Are they nice, supportive, kind, understanding, loyal, loving, and accountable?

Sometimes we try so hard to fit into a group of people that we even start to change ourselves. We do things we don't even want to do, we start talking a certain way, or dressing a certain way. We might even try to change the way we look with the hopes of fitting in with this group of people. We've all been there, I promise. This has happened to everyone! Sometimes friends and friendships aren't meant to happen. Sometimes they aren't meant to last forever and that's okay. Because sadly, even all of the friendship bracelets and BFF necklaces in the world aren't strong enough to keep two people, or a group of people together, who just aren't meant to be together.

I'm going to be honest with you - I am not someone who has confidence bursting out of me like shimmering glitter. But I do choose to work on it every day and I can tell you that I have so much more confidence in myself now than I did in middle school or high school. And, I hope that as I grow up I become even more confident in myself. And with this confidence, I have learned and reevaluated the treatment that I deserve, as well as not feeling the urge to hangout with 'friends' who treat me more like an enemy. Thinking back...I can actually think of several stories where I wish I would have had more confidence in myself, and felt less pressure to try to force a friendship or relationship to work. There are two of these stories that really stand out as important lessons to me - and I want to share those stories with you.

* * *

Story one: That one time my friends broke up with me...

I was a sophomore? No, junior? Anyways - I was in my sophomore or junior year of highschool when my two 'best friends' decided that they no longer wanted me to be a part of their friend group. I still am not 100% sure on why they no longer wanted me to be the third amigo - the only reason they gave me was that they felt 'it just wasn't working anymore' and they 'no longer wanted me to be a part of the group'. It was awful. I had been friends with these girls since grade school and here they were abruptly kicking me to the curb. Honestly, it still makes me sad whenever I think about it...

It was a school night, a Tuesday night I think...I had just gotten home from basketball practice. Obviously I was super sweaty, tired, and gross. I also had a huge Algebra 2 test the next day that I really needed to study for...the Lord unfortunately did not bless me with the ability to understand the majority of math. So you could definitely say that it was my weakest and least favorite subject. It's okay though...

So picture it - there I am sitting at the kitchen table studying while my step mom was making dinner. I hadn't showered yet - I was going to wait and do that after dinner - I thought this would be a good way to continue my procrastination of studying for my upcoming test. All of a sudden my phone dings...yes! I thought. A welcomed distraction! I learned quickly that this wasn't the case...I had a text from my best friend Rachel "Hey, Keri. Sarah and I are outside. We want to talk to you..." Wait what? I was so confused. And yes - this is the same Rachel that was my BFF from the 8th grade pool party.

Something that's important to know here - my friend Sarah actually lived down the street from my step mom and dad's house. So this wasn't a huge shock that they were out front - they easily could have walked to my house. The shock was that they were here, together, uninvited, and I had no prep time to get ready for whatever was about to unfold.

I excused myself from studying at the kitchen table while everyone else was getting ready to eat dinner. I told everyone that Sarah and Rachel were outside and they must have wanted to stop by to say hello! I opened the garage and walked outside ready to greet my friends "Hey guys! We're actually just about to eat dinner? You guys want to come inside and eat?" Sarah remained pretty quiet through the whole exchange...but Rachel started off by coldly saying "no, um we'd actually just like to talk to you out here. So you can sit down." Something was up...and I didn't have a CLUE as to what was about to happen. As we all sat in the driveway, Rachel and Sarah went on to explain that they no longer wanted to be friends with me.

Here are my two best friends telling me that they no longer want to be my friend!? I couldn't understand it! I pleaded...I begged for explanations, or some insight, or any examples of things that I had done that might have caused them to not want to be friends with me anymore. I sat there thinking that the whole thing was my fault - my fault.

Let that sink in a bit. Here I was on a school night, exhausted, studying for a test in my worst subject, missing dinner with my family, and out of the blue my two 'friends' rudely show up uninvited - just to tell me how I'm 'not good enough' and how they've 'outgrown me' and that they 'just don't want me to be in the friend group anymore'. All with zero examples of why or any given explanations. I was heartbroken. I was sitting there crying on the driveway in front of them and they weren't comforting me or saying anything other than 'but don't worry...we'll still say hi to you in the hallways at school and stuff.' Like WOW! What a blessing that is! Seriously?!

And as I was sitting there - I found myself questioning anything and everything that I had ever done and trying to find examples and reasons of how this might have been my fault. That there must be something wrong with me, or that I wasn't good enough to be friends with them.

The me now wishes I would have said something like "Okay, fine! Who needs friends like you guys. I deserve better than to be treated like this. Thanks for letting me know. Goodnight." But unfortunately, at the time, all I could do was silently stand up, and go inside while beginning to cry uncontrollably to my family about how my two best friends no longer want to be my friend...

I wish I would have known at the time that this wasn't my fault. I wish I would have known that it's okay to no longer be in this friend group - even if it was scary because I wasn't 'best friends' with anyone else. I wish I would have realized the fact that they were toxic friends and that I deserved to be treated better. I didn't know all of that then, but I wanted to share this story with you so that you know this now.

I didn't deserve to be treated like that. Especially by my so-called 'friends'. I wish I would have had the confidence in my-self then to be okay with the friendship ending and to not be so fearful of the unknown. I wish I would have known then that everything happens for a reason - and that it's all going to be okay - even when it seems like your world is crumbling right in front of you.

Another story that I want to share with you is the time that I let a guy choose between me and another girl...

* * *

Story two: That one time when the guy made a 'pro' and 'con' list about me...

Oh how I wish that this wasn't a story that was a part of my life...but it is and I am embracing it. Picture me in 8th grade...wearing my glorious black and red track uniform (hello track tans!) hair pulled back into a high pony-tail with red pre-wrap as a headband, my lucky socks and my blue and grey Asics running shoes. I was so ready for this track meet!

While we were waiting in the bleachers for our next event to be called (my next event was the 4x4 relay) Blye was texting me...he was like so cute, and athletic, and super sweet. I had a huge crush on him and wanted nothing more than to be his girlfriend. - As I write this I am internally screaming at my cringe-worthy younger self...but it's true.

As we were texting and wishing one another luck in our up-coming events (he did the 4x2 and high-jump) he wanted to let me know that he really liked me...but there was another girl in 7th grade who he also liked and he wanted to be "totally honest" with me and let me know that he was deciding between the two of us. And that he needed to make a 'pro' and 'con' list of the two of us.

And you better believe that I was sitting there hoping with all of my heart that he would choose me. That I would be the luckiest girl ever if he chose me. Oh how I wanted him to choose me! Then comes the announcement over the loud-speaker calling for the girls 4x4 to head down to the track to get ready - my daydreaming of my relationship with Blye had to wait until after the race.

* * *

We won! My team got first in the 4x4! We were all so excited. I couldn't wait to get back to the bleachers and be celebrated by all of my other teammates on our successful victory! Once I was able to settle down and wait for my next event, I became really excited to check my phone to see if Blye had texted me to let me know what his decision was...I took out my phone and I had 2 new text messages...both from Blye! First winning the race, now this! What a great day!

The smile on my face immediately vanished once I opened the texts...to this day I still remember some of what was said. The texts went something like...

"Hi Keri. I wanted to let you know that I've chosen Kaite (the other girl). After making my list I just think she's better. But you're still really nice! And I hope we can be friends." He then had the nerve to type out and send me the 'pro' and 'con' list that he created about me that helped him make his decision:

Pros:
nice/sweet
pretty
doesn't wear a lot of makeup
athletic

funny

Cons:
too clumsy
legs are too long (butt is too high off of the ground)
weird stomach
too shy

My heart sank when I read these things. I felt so hurt. I remember feeling so defeated, so small and totally inadequate. The first text of him choosing Katie was enough...and he thought that sending me this list would make me feel better? The situation only got worse when my friend Christian (yes same Christian from the pool party) told me that he had made this list collectively with a few other guys in our grade...guys who I thought were my friends. Ouch...

Katie and Blye would go on to date for a few weeks and then broke up right before summer.

* * *

I wish I would have had the courage and confidence back then that I do now. I wish I would have taken myself out of the 'decision' all together. Once Blye texted me that he was deciding between me and another girl, I wish I would have known my worth and replied "you know what...I'll make it easy on you. I'm no longer an option." But I didn't...because I didn't think I was worth being someone's first and only choice.

I wish I didn't go home that night and stand in front of my mirror and ask myself "are my legs too long?" "Is my butt too high?" "Why does everything think I have a weird stomach?". I remember looking so intensely at myself - trying to figure it all out - And I just couldn't figure it out! It didn't make sense! Why was I being judged by others on how *my* body looked? Why did these boys feel like they could say these things so bluntly towards me? What gave them the right? I never said anything about their bodies to them - I was never so direct and rude to them. Why were they being this way to me? I was going around and around in circles and couldn't figure it out. I showered, put on my pajamas, and went to bed.

* * *

Don't give others the power to make yourself feel small. Don't give others the power to make you think your body should look a certain way, or that your personality should be different. They don't get to say those things about you! They have no right. All that matters is how you feel about yourself. Give yourself the power to know that you're good enough. Give yourself the power to know that your body is yours and it's perfect the way it is. Give yourself the power to know that you deserve to be happy and fully love yourself and to have someone that loves you unconditionally, the way you are. Give yourself the power to know that you are a goddess - and deserve nothing less.

Chapter Ten Reflections

Do you have a friend(s) who can be toxic and make you feel bad? If so, who?

What steps can you take to try to distance yourself from them?

Do you think you would be happier if you didn't hangout with them as often? Why or why not?

Do you currently give people the power to change how you feel or how you feel about yourself?

How can you give them less power?

What are three things you love about your personality?

1.

2.

3.

What are three things you love about your body?

1.

2.

3.

What are three things you love about you?

1.

2.

3.

FINAL THOUGHTS - WHAT I HOPE YOU TAKE WITH YOU

You made it to the end! Congrats...that's a big accomplishment! When I was your age I wasn't a 'big reader' so I still get excited anytime I finish a book. And now that you have finished, I want to leave you with a few things...

I hope that you make a promise to yourself that you're going to continue to work on becoming confident in yourself, your abilities, and who you are as a person. You must believe me when I tell you that you are amazing. You are like no one else on this entire planet! Please see that as something incredible. I want you to continue to practice loving and accepting yourself. And to vow that you will work on doing things that bring you joy throughout your life. You deserve happiness and you deserve finding that happiness in your truest self.

I hope that you take your new creations of confidence to inspire you to follow your dreams! You have your whole life ahead of you, and there are going to be so many wonderful experiences and things that come your way. I want you to chase down your dreams - and know that no dream is too big. Work on having confidence in yourself and your abilities and using this to fuel your pursuit of whatever you want to be, whatever you want to do, and how you want to live your life. You can do anything that you put your mind to - and I want you to take the first step in your journey today by beginning to see how amazing and capable you are today - through your own eyes.

I am one who believes that we all have a path in life that is unique to each of us. Of course, there are certain things that we can do that can change the courses of this path. But I do believe that we all have a calling. It's up to you to be open to your calling. And becoming comfortable and confident enough with yourself to have the courage to find and accept your calling. Know that in this pursuit you will sometimes fail. But failure is not a bad thing! In fact, you should openly welcome failure. It means that you're learning and growing! Say it with me... "failure is not a bad thing. It means I am learning and growing." Just keep practicing. Keep having faith and confidence in yourself. And continue to tell yourself that you can do this. And, above all else - know that you are all of these things and more:

- You are loved
- You are valued
- You are strong
- You are smart
- You are courageous

- You are beautiful inside and out
- You are kind
- You are a good person
- You can do this
- You deserve happiness

Now go forward into the world loving yourself, being confident in who you are, and knowing that the world is a better place because you are in it.

Keri Cook is a captivating writer who has channeled her passion for the empowerment of young women into a refreshing and relatable piece of literature, *The Little Blue Book*. Months before her graduation from Missouri State University in 2018, she discovered a gleaming pull to mentor and empower young women from her hometown of Springfield, Missouri through a local organization, The Circle for Girls Foundation. In addition to her time spent mentoring, Keri was actively involved in substitute teaching at various schools and experiencing first hand the issues and topics that middle and high school aged students were desperately seeking to know more about. It was through her work at the foundation, as well as her time spent teaching, that Keri discovered how critical it is to encourage young women to become confident in themselves and their abilities. She quickly learned that this passion of hers was one that she wanted to propel even further. So, after graduation, she moved to Washington, D.C. where she was able to work for the Close Up Foundation, an organization who works to inform, inspire, and empower young people from across the country to become more actively engaged citizens. Through these experiences, she became inspired to share these lessons with young women everywhere.